FOR GOD SO LOVED THE WORLD

Looking at Life Through Faith-colored Glasses

FOR GOD SO LOVED THE WORLD

Looking at Life Through Faith-colored Glasses

FRANK C. RAY, IV

For God so Loved the World
Looking at Life Through Faith-colored Glasses

by

Frank C. Ray, IV

Published by Frank C. Ray, IV
https://pcguyiv.wordpress.com/about-me/contact-me/

All portions of this work after the preface were blog entries on *Thoughts & Theories* (https://pcguyiv.wordpress.com/), the author's personal blog, written under the screen name, PCGuyIV.

All Scripture references are from the King James Version, which is in the public domain.

Book and cover design by Frank C. Ray, IV

Globe and Glasses cover art created by Frank C. Ray, IV by combining public domain images of the Earth and eyeglasses that are free to use and modify for either personal or commercial purposes.

Special thanks to Mark Adkinson for his assistance editing the final draft.

Printed in the United States by Kindle Direct Publishing

Paperback ISBN: 979-8-9900409-0-8
E-Book ISBN: 979-8-9900409-2-2

For my wife, Donna,
who helped me find my faith.

Now faith is the substance of things hoped for,
the evidence of things not seen.
– Hebrews 11:1

TABLE OF CONTENTS

PREFACE

ACK IN THE early 2000s, I began blogging. At some point, I started a blog entitled *For God so Loved the World*. The sole purpose of this blog was to be a place where I could put my observations and thoughts about my personal faith and Christianity in general in writing.

Around 2005, the blogging service I was using shut down, so I moved most of the contents from that blog to my primary blog. I grouped all the posts under one category named after my original site. I continued to add to it periodically until May of 2023, when I decided to remove all posts from my blog and start fresh.

Being the sentimental person that I am, I didn't just wipe the slate clean without thought or care for all the hard work I put into my blog. I made a backup copy of all my posts on a private blog so that I could reference them if I ever felt the need. This book is the direct result of that need.

Each entry in this book began as a post on my blog, *Thoughts & Theories*, under the category "For God so Loved the World". Most of them have been edited, either to correct typographical and grammatical errors that I didn't catch originally or to better reflect the thought that I was attempting to convey. Some titles have also been updated to better reflect the contents of the post.

I don't claim to be a great theological scholar, nor do I have any degrees from seminary or any kind of clerical title. What I do have is a personal relationship with Jesus Christ, and as a follower of Christ, I present this compilation of my blog posts to share my personal views of faith and Christianity with others.

* * *

ONE THING YOU'LL notice as you read through this book is that all Scripture references are taken from the King James Version (KJV) of the Bible. The KJV may seem to be an outdated translation to many, and there are plenty of other translations to choose from, so you might be wondering why I chose to use it rather than a more modern translation. There are two key reasons: personal preference and copyright.

The reason I prefer the KJV over most other versions is quite simple: familiarity. It's what I grew up with, and it was the required translation of the private high school I graduated from. I'm not one of those who touts the KJV as the only legitimate translation of the Bible, but it is a good translation. I had considered switching to the New King James Version (NKJV), as it is very similar to the KJV but replaces many of the archaic word forms with modern ones. This makes it much easier to read, but copyright concerns prompted me to go with the original KJV that I used when writing the posts for my blog.

PEW POTATOES

THE CHRISTIAN LIFE is not a sedentary one. As believers, God's Word frequently calls us to action. The Great Commission (Matthew 28:19–20) is probably the best-known example of this. Even the Great Commandments (Matthew 22:37–40) are not passive in nature. Worship, prayer, and praise also require active participation. So why do we often sit back and do nothing, just waiting for Sunday to show up?

Sometimes we struggle to know what God wants us to do. If we are honest, this is usually a sign that we've gotten too caught up in the cares of this world, and our daily walk has fallen by the wayside. We've become pew potatoes filling our seats on Sunday morning, rooted there by complacency, quite comfortable with our lack of any real spiritual involvement in the church.

God wants us to participate in His work. We go to church and Bible study to be equipped to live for Him. But only by living in obedience to God on a daily basis can we avoid becoming pew potatoes.

But be ye doers of the word, and not hearers only, deceiving your own selves. For if any be a hearer of the word, and not a doer, he is like unto a man beholding his natural face in a glass: For he beholdeth himself, and goeth his way, and straightway forgetteth what manner of man he was. But whoso looketh into the perfect law of liberty, and continueth therein, he being not a forgetful hearer, but a doer of the work, this man shall be blessed in his deed.

– JAMES 1:22–25

OF MOTES AND BEAMS

THE NEW TESTAMENT speaks repeatedly about lovingly correcting those believers who have wandered astray; however, there is a distinct difference between loving correction and being judgmental. It's easy to become judgmental, especially under the guise of church discipline. We either say to ourselves that we're better than that or we criticize the parts of their lives we disagree with, citing our supposed concern for their soul as our justification. Regardless of why we are being judgmental or how we try to justify it, it goes against the words of Christ: "Judge not, that ye be not judged. For with that what judgment ye judge, ye shall be judged; and with what measure ye mete, it shall be measured to you again." (Matthew 7:1–2)

When we rush to judgment, it's often because we see a flaw in someone else that we ourselves possess. Christ Himself put it best: "And why beholdest thou the mote that is in thy brother's eye, but consider not the beam that is in thine own eye? Or how wilt thou say to thy brother, Let me pull out the mote out of thine eye, and behold, a beam is in thine own eye? Thou hypocrite, first cast out the beam that is in thine own eye; and then shalt thou see clearly to cast out the mote out of thy brother's eye." (Matthew 7:3–5) Perhaps if we would take the time to honestly evaluate our own lives in the light of God's Word, we might find it easier to not be so quick to judge. We might also find that the problem we see in the other person lies with us.

> *Therefore thou art inexcusable, O man, whosoever thou art that judgest: for wherein thou judgest another, thou condemnest thyself; for thou that judgest doest the same things.*
>
> – ROMANS 2:1

JUST ONE FRUIT

YOU'VE LIKELY HEARD of the "fruits" of the Spirit found in Galatians, but if you read carefully, that's not completely accurate. The list found in Galatians isn't a list of different fruits but rather a list of the different components of one single fruit. Galatians 5:22 starts off with, "The fruit of the Spirit..." Love, joy, peace, longsuffering, etc. are all parts of one fruit of the Spirit, not individual fruits. None of us are perfect at showing all these attributes, but as Christians, each of these areas should develop over time.

As a single fruit, these different attributes are inseparable; they intermingle and build on each other. The qualities necessary to bring forth one can only be found among the others. Though we frequently view these attributes as independent of each other, according to God's Word, they are parts of the whole. It would be incorrect to state that each individual believer is a separate body of Christ. Christ doesn't have many bodies; He has one body: the Church, of which every believer is a part. In the same way, there are not multiple fruits of the Spirit, just multiple parts of one fruit.

> *But the fruit of the Spirit is love, joy, longsuffering, gentleness, goodness, faith, meekness, temperance: against such there is no law.*
>
> — GALATIANS 5:22–23

MEMORIAL DAY

HERE IN THE US, Memorial Day is always the last Monday in May, and for many, Memorial Day weekend serves as the kick-off for the summer season, even though summer itself doesn't officially begin until almost three weeks later. Sadly, the true significance of Memorial Day is frequently overlooked. It is supposed to be a time to remember and honor those who gave their lives serving our country.

As Christians, we have our own "Memorial Day". That day is Easter. It's when we celebrate and remember what God did for us through the sacrifice and resurrection of His Son, Jesus Christ. Jesus Himself, though, gave us instructions to remember on a regular basis. Communion (or the Lord's Supper, depending on your denominational affiliation) was given to us by Jesus Christ as a way to remember Him and what He did. So, the next time you take communion, try thinking of it as your "Memorial Day" celebration for the Lord.

And He took bread, and gave thanks, and brake it, and gave unto them, saying, This is My body which is given for you: this do in remembrance of Me. Likewise also the cup after supper, saying, This cup is the new testament in My blood, which is shed for you.

– LUKE 22:19–20

BEING FRUITFUL

And when he saw a fig tree in the way, he came to it,
and found nothing thereon, but leaves only, and said
unto it, Let no fruit grow on thee henceforward for
ever. And presently the fig tree withered away.
— MATTHEW 21:19

DID YOU KNOW that, as Christians, we are supposed to bear fruit? When Jesus cursed the fig tree, it wasn't out of anger at being unable to eat; rather, it was because the barren tree was worthless as a fig tree. In the same way, a Christian who does not produce fruit—Godly works—is also useless. This may sound harsh, but Jesus Himself states this quite clearly: "I am the true vine, and my Father is the husbandman. Every branch in me that beareth not fruit he taketh away..." (John 15:1–2a)

This does not mean that works will save you. As Paul wrote, "For by grace are ye saved through faith; and that not of yourselves: it is the gift of God: not of works, lest any man should boast." (Ephesians 2:8–9) Our works are, however, evidence of our faith. This is the reason James states that faith without works is dead (James 2:16–20). As if this were not enough, Jesus' warning to the church at Sardis should spur us to good works: "...I know thy works, that thou hast a name that thou livest, and art dead. Be watchful, and strengthen the things which remain, that are ready to die: for I have not found thy works perfect before God. Remember therefore how thou has received and heard, and hold fast, and repent. If therefore thou shalt not watch, I will come on thee as a thief, and thou shalt not know what hour I will come upon thee." (Revelation 3:1b–3)

Time grows short, and there is much yet to be done for the Kingdom of God. Let us be about His perfect and holy work, producing fruit while we still can. While it is not our salvation, it should be our desire.

A God of Second Chances?

GOD IS VERY patient with us. Being the fallible humans that we are, we often make mistakes or miss opportunities, but God is there, ready and willing to forgive and provide another opportunity. He even waits patiently for non-believers to come to Him. II Peter 3:9 says, "The Lord is not slack concerning his promise, as some men count slackness; but is longsuffering to us-ward, not willing that any should perish, but that all should come to repentance." As such, it is often said that God is a God of second chances, but is that truly accurate?

While this life may be replete with opportunities for non-believers to repent and accept the redemptive work of Christ and for believers to take every opportunity to spread the gospel, once this life is over, there are no more chances. God's Word is as clear on this as it is regarding His patience: "And as it is appointed unto men once to die, but after this the judgment:" (Hebrews 9:27). Once we die, no further opportunity is given. If we haven't accepted Christ in this life, there won't be a second chance going into the next.

INDEPENDENCE DAY

EVERY YEAR ON July 4th, here in the United States, we celebrate our nation's independence from British rule. There is, however, another Independence Day in the life of every Christian that is unique to each believer. It is the day they accepted Christ.

Until someone accepts Jesus Christ as Lord and Savior, that person is in servitude to sin. God's Word states, "For the wages of sin is death..." (Romans 6:23a) In other words, if you aren't free from sin, then you will spend an eternity separated from God. God is holy and cannot allow a sinful person to enter His presence.

The good news is, as every true believer knows, that God provided a way to escape servitude to sin and spend eternity in heaven with Him rather than in hell. The rest of Romans 6:23 tells us, "...the gift of God is eternal life through Jesus Christ our Lord." All we must do is believe in Jesus Christ, and we will be saved. Faith in Jesus is the only way to receive this gift and escape the eternal consequences of our sin. "Neither is there salvation in any other: for there is none other name under heaven given among men, whereby we must be saved." (Acts 4:12)

The final question is this: have you had your own personal Independence Day?

> *Then said Jesus to those Jews which believed on him, If you continue in my word, then ye are my disciples indeed, and ye shall know the truth, and the truth shall make you free. They answered him, We be Abraham's seed, and were never in bondage to any man: how sayest thou, Ye shall be made free? Jesus answered them, Verily, verily, I say unto you, whosoever committeth sin is the servant of sin. And the servant abideth not in the house for ever; but the Son abideth ever. If the Son therefore shall make you free, ye shall be free indeed.*

– JOHN 8:31–36

TOO MUCH CLUTTER

HAVE YOU EVER noticed how everything starts out nice and clean in your home, but over time, things begin to pile up? Unless you do your daily chores and keep things tidy, eventually the place gets cluttered. An interesting thing about clutter is that not everything that becomes clutter is necessarily junk. In some cases, it's just out of place. A dining room table covered in books is useless. The books aren't trash; they're just in the wrong place. A couch covered in clothes isn't very easy to sit on, but the clothes aren't trash; they're just in the wrong place.

Of course, sometimes clutter comes from not having a place to put everything. Normally, this is a result of having too much stuff. When you've filled up all your storage and all the reorganizing in the world doesn't make a place for everything, then you have too much stuff, and that extra stuff becomes clutter.

Our homes aren't the only things that can become cluttered. As with not doing daily chores, if we aren't daily seeking God and renewing our walk with Him, our lives become too busy and cluttered. We become encumbered by the cares of this world, ensnared by those weights and sins that, as the author of Hebrews wrote, so easily beset us. (Hebrews 12:1)

Just as we can clutter up our homes by leaving books on the dining room table and clothes on the couch, we can clutter up our lives by doing too much. If we fill our lives with so much church work that other parts of our lives suffer, then we have cluttered up our lives with church work. Every believer has a part to play in the church, but not every believer is to play every part. We must ask God to show us our place in the church and not take on more than what we are called to do. God promises to enable us to do all that He calls us to do, but taking on more than what we are called to do just adds clutter.

Just as doing daily chores and making sure things are put back in their places keeps our homes clean and uncluttered, making time for God and seeking His will in what we do helps us to maintain a sinless, uncluttered life.

> *But seek ye first the kingdom of God, and his righteousness; and all these things shall be added unto you.*
>
> – MATTHEW 6:33

CHRISTIAN SPAM

OF ALL THE spam I get in my email or see on social media, the ones I hate the most are what I refer to as Christian spam. It's those sappy, sentimental messages you get from well-intended friends and family that have some variant of the following message: "I love Jesus. Do you love Jesus? If you love Jesus, share this message with ten people, including the person who shared it with you; otherwise, you don't love Jesus, and Jesus won't love you."

When I first started getting these, my initial reaction was to do exactly as the message suggested, but then I realized that these were nothing more than traditional chain mail spam given a religious whitewash. I certainly didn't want them junking up my inbox or feed, so why would I send such garbage to someone else?

You may be wondering what the problem with these emails is. To begin with, the nature of these emails is to make you feel guilty or fear that you won't be saved if you don't act on them. This is the classic fear tactic used by all chain letters to some degree or another, but there is another fault with these messages that is a greater issue. In fact, it's the most important reason that we, as believers, should all do our part to stop the spread of these messages.

If you look closely at most of these messages, you will notice that the sense of security offered comes only if you continue the chain by either forwarding the email or sharing the post and tagging others. Scripture is clear: we only gain salvation by grace through faith and not by works (Ephesians 2:8–9). We can do nothing to earn our salvation; however, these emails and posts tell a different story. According to these messages, all someone must do to be saved is continue the chain, thus proving their love for God and Jesus. While it may seem like a far-fetched leap of logic, human nature lends itself to believing you must do something to earn salvation. As responsible Christians, the only salvation message we should be propagating is the one found in the Bible.

> *But though we, or an angel from heaven, preach any other gospel unto you than that which we have preached unto you, let him be accursed. As we said before, so say I now again, If any man preach any other gospel unto you than that ye have received, let him be accursed.*
>
> – GALATIANS 1:8–9

HIGHWAY HYPOCRISY

COMEDIANS LOVE TO point out all the horrible drivers that have Christian-themed decals, bumper stickers, license plates, and ornaments on their cars. When I say *horrible drivers*, I'm not talking about those who aren't skilled at driving but rather those who have a flagrant disregard of courteous, polite, and, in many cases, legal handling of their vehicles; the ones whose road rage, self-centered attitude, or both have such a glare that it dims any light of Christianity their automobiles attempt to show. It may be that some have purchased a used car, and those items were placed on the car by the previous owner. To those individuals, I say, "Please remove those items from your car." For the majority of others, though, I also say, "Please remove those items from your car." The reason is simple: they're playing the hypocrite.

Our actions don't save us, but our salvation should alter our actions. We should not be like the world. Others will believe the truth of our actions before they'll believe the truth of our words. While some view plastering their cars with Christian paraphernalia as an action, the world views it as talk. Like wearing a Christian t-shirt or baseball cap, it's a nonverbal way of telling others that we are followers of Christ, but it's what the world sees reflected in our actions that lets them know we mean business. It's better not to announce our faith and live like Christians than to proclaim to be believers and live like the world.

> *Yea, a man may say, Thou has faith, and I have works: shew me thy faith without works, and I will shew thee my faith by my works.*
>
> – JAMES 2:18

THE WAYWARD SHEEP

FAR TOO OFTEN, I get wrapped up in the daily grind and personal ambitions. I will, for a season, let my focus drift off of Jesus and onto the cares and worries of this life. My personal Bible study and prayer time are ignored, and as a result, I suffer for it. Feelings of anxiety and stress that were previously removed find their way back into my life.

There are two reasons I bring this up. First, confession is good for the soul. Admitting sins and flaws is the first step toward repentance and, thereby, forgiveness and salvation. Second, it serves as a reminder that no matter how far I've come, it's always possible to take up, rather than lay aside, those sins that so easily beset us (Hebrews 12:1).

This sort of thing happens to everyone from time to time. There are no perfect people in this world. The question is, when we stumble, how do we respond? Do we admit our sin, repent, and start again, following the path God has set before us, or do we wallow in self-pity or revel in our transgressions? Jesus makes it clear in

Matthew 18 that God wants us to come back to Him when we stray. Even the Psalmist states that he chooses to return to God after wandering away (Psalm 119:169–176). The only real choice for any believer should be obvious. There is no room in the Christian life for self-pity or love of sin.

> *I beseech you therefore, brethren, by the mercies of God, that you present your bodies a living sacrifice, holy, acceptable unto God, which is your reasonable service. And be not conformed to this world: but be ye transformed by the renewing of your mind, that ye may prove what is that good, and acceptable, and perfect, will of God.*
>
> – Romans 12:1–2

SENDING THE WRONG MESSAGE

ONCE AGAIN, I received more Christian spam from well-meaning individuals. This time, it was an email regarding a certain television network, a certain Christian talk-show host, a particular atheist activist, and the long-since canceled TV show *Touched by an Angel*. The email instructed me to add my name and forward it to everyone in my address book. Well, I didn't do that, though at least one of my reasons might surprise you.

First, this was clearly a chain letter. This reason alone was enough to keep me from forwarding it, though it was far from the most compelling reason. Next, the story told in the email had been discredited. Despite what the email stated, there was no connection between either of the individuals mentioned and the network's decision to cancel the show. It had run its course and was losing viewership. It was only natural that the network would cancel it. Also, when I received the email, the show had been off the air for quite some time, so why would anyone still care? My final reason, though, was the most compelling: I was glad and grateful the show was off the air.

It may seem odd that someone professing to believe in God would want such an obviously faith-based show off the air, but, in reality, all true Christians should have been the ones trying to get the show canceled. *Touched by an Angel* never once mentioned Jesus Christ as the way to salvation. What was presented on the show was a watered-down, sanitized, Christless, so-called gospel. Jesus Himself said, "I am the way, the truth, and the life: no man cometh unto the Father, but by me." (John 14:6b) Any gospel contrary to that presented in God's Holy Word, no matter how religion-shellacked it may be, is heresy, and those who spread it are to be counted as cursed.

> *But though we, or an angel from heaven, preach any other gospel unto you than that which we have preached unto you, let him be accursed. As we said before, so say I now again, If any man preach any other gospel unto you than that ye have received, let him be accursed.*
>
> – GALATIANS 1:8–9

APATHY AND THE CAGED LION

WHEN SOMEONE SAYS, "He's like a caged lion," apathy isn't necessarily the first thing that comes to mind. Instead, we likely envision a highly agitated beast pacing back and forth, snarling, testing the bars for weak points, accompanied by the occasional angry roar. But that is from a lion recently caged. What of the lion long imprisoned?

Today, a captive lion is likely a zoo resident. He's been captive for so long that he hardly remembers freedom. It's even possible that he was born in captivity. He doesn't pace or test his enclosure for a way out. Absent are the snarls and angry roars. Instead of a fierce predator, we are faced with what appears to be no more than a docile, overgrown housecat who only reminds us of his imposing grandeur when mealtime comes around. While he may still long for the thrill of hunting down a zebra or gazelle in his inward-most being, and while he is still far from tame or domesticated, the years of captivity have rendered him apathetic toward his current condition.

Much like the lion, many of us are apathetic toward our current condition. After many attempts to chase after our dreams and aspirations, only to have them come crashing down, we no longer care to test the bars of our monotonous and uninspiring existence, and so we are sentenced, as Henry David Thorough once said, "lives of quiet desperation". We have settled for the mediocre, and in some cases, the less than mediocre, and given up on something greater. This goes against what Christ taught: "I am come that they might have life, and that they might have it more abundantly." (John 10:10b)

Too often, we are perfectly content to wallow in less than what God has in store for us, simply because our current situation is familiar and comfortable, and we have grown apathetic toward aspiring to something greater. Abundant life only comes as we follow God and His perfect will for our lives, and that is seldom if ever comfortable or familiar, and it certainly isn't apathetic. We must get out of ourselves, shake off apathy, and leave the confines of the comfortable and familiar so we can live up to God's calling. The reward for doing so is far greater than the pablum this world has to offer.

OF GRAVEN IMAGES

Thou shalt not make unto thee any graven image, or any likeness of any thing that is in heaven above, or that is in the earth beneath, or that is in the water under the earth: thou shalt not bow down thyself to them, nor serve them: for I the LORD thy God am a jealous God, visiting the iniquity of the fathers upon the children unto the third and fourth generations of them that hate me; and showing mercy unto thousands of them that love me, and keep my commandments.

– EXODUS 20:4–6

MANY VIEW THE second commandment as merely a reiteration of the first, and while this interpretation is understandable, it isn't accurate. The first and second commandments often go hand in hand, but it is quite possible to make graven images without the intent of worshiping other gods. In fact, it's quite possible to take otherwise important and holy symbols and turn them into graven images.

First, we must have a clear understanding of exactly what a graven image is. Yes, it can be what we typically think of as an idol or icon: a statue, image, or figurine representing a deity, typically placed in a temple or shrine. More importantly, though, it can be anything physical that we perceive as required to worship or to which we ascribe the powers of God. Talismans and charms fall into this category.

The Israelites decided while Moses was still up on the mountain receiving the Ten Commandments that they needed a golden calf to represent the gods who brought them out of Egypt (Exodus 32:1–6), violating both the First and Second Commandments. Even if they had decided that the statue represented the one true living God, it still violated the Second Commandment.

Even the most sacred of artifacts to the Israelites became a graven image when it was used as a talisman. When the Ark of the Covenant was brought before the army of Israel, normally it was to show their allegiance to and reliance on God, but when it was brought forth simply to serve as a protective talisman, supposedly harboring the power of God, Israel was defeated, and the Ark was captured by the Philistines (I Samuel 4:3–11).

While the Bible is God's Word, we should not treat the physical book in the same fashion as Israel treated the Ark. We should not hang or carry crosses as spiritual talismans. If we carry or display any item expecting it to either possess or provide us with God's power or somehow connect us with God simply by having it with us, we have done nothing more than turn that item, no matter how seemingly holy, spiritual, sacred, or religious it may be, into a graven image.

GOD'S WISDOM

MY WIFE AND I received a new devotional for Christmas and started reading through it on January 1st. So far, I've been impressed. It's one of those that is set up to be read through in a year, thus our choice of beginning on New Year's Day rather than immediately after Christmas. The main premise of the devotional is focusing on the wisdom of God, and it's made some interesting points, the most poignant of which, at least for me, is that God's wisdom and God's direction are not the same thing.

The message of the devotional is that we should ask for God's wisdom rather than His direction. Receiving direction doesn't require a relationship with God, at least not the deep kind of relationship that God wants us to have and that we should desire. Asking for wisdom, though, requires being attentive to what He says and investing our time in truly seeking His aid in our decision-making process.

The best analogy that I can come up with is that of a student and a teacher. When you ask a teacher about an assignment, he doesn't give you the answer but rather gives you the methods and tools necessary to reason your way through the problem. In much the same way, asking for God's direction is like asking for the answer to the problem. Asking for His wisdom, however, is asking Him to provide us with the tools and methods to be able to discern what He would have us to do.

I am certainly guilty of asking for the answers, not that there is anything particularly wrong with that. I think there are times in our faith that asking for the answer is necessary, and God is willing to give us that answer to bolster our faith. However, God wants us to have a much deeper relationship with Him, and asking for His wisdom rather than His direction doesn't just require that kind of relationship; it helps establish and maintain it as well.

LINUX FOR CHRISTIANS?

I AM A computer nerd at heart. Over the course of my existence, I have written programs, designed web pages, and worked on computers both as a hobby and as a profession, including building "new" machines out of spare parts from older machines. At one point in time, I had five working computers in my home, and only one of them ran Windows. The rest ran Linux in some form or fashion. I tell you this to provide insight as to why I found the concept of Linux for Christians interesting and to give some clue as to why I would even run across it.

While searching for a new version of Linux to replace my once-favorite distribution, I came across, quite by accident, two websites. The first was regarding a Linux distribution called *Ichthux*. It was, in essence, a variant of *Ubuntu* with different desktop artwork and a specialized software selection rather than a truly unique and separate distribution, but it touted itself as "Linux for Christians". I have two issues with this. First and foremost, it implies that Linux in and of itself isn't for

Christians. An operating system, much like the computer that it runs on, is amoral—neither good nor evil. It's how we use it that matters. Second, when I first went to the website, I was under the impression that it was a unique Linux distribution in and of itself, and such was not the case. Along with being put off by what I perceived as a misrepresentation of the product, I questioned if an operating system aimed at Christians was even truly necessary.

In continuing my search for a new distribution, I ran across a page that was titled *Linux for Christians*. Considering my initial discovery, I was hesitant to even give the page a second glance, but I'm glad I did. Rather than presenting a distribution or package set aimed at Christians, it discussed using Linux in a Christian environment and being a Christian using Linux. It provided information on Bible study software and various other programs usable by individuals, churches, and other religious organizations. I also liked the site's slogan: "Linux – Free, as in Salvation. Eph 2:8–9". (A rather neat twist on the usual Linux slogan.) While this site didn't solve my search for a new distribution, it did provide some useful information.

There are three things my search for a new Linux version confirmed for me. First, all tools—computers and operating systems included—are only good or evil based on how they are used. Second, we need to seek God's wisdom in discerning how to use the things He has given us to make sure we use them for good and His glory. And third, we can then share His imparted wisdom with others who have similar questions or issues.

READ ANY GOOD BOOK LATELY?

H E'S READ HUNDREDS of devotionals, topical studies, Sunday school lessons, and commentaries from several highly respected Christian authors. He's attended church every Sunday that he possibly could. If he did miss a Sunday, he got a sermon on tape on Wednesday night. But he's never once cracked the cover of that huge study Bible he carries with him, or any Bible for that matter.

I'm certain that we've all known someone like this, and it's sad that some people go through life this way, thinking they know what God says about things simply because they've read about the Bible, listened to others talk about the Bible, and gone to the trouble of owning at least one Bible. The problem is that when it comes to what God says, second-hand information just isn't up to His standard.

We are admonished again and again to know what God says. How can we do this if we don't read His word for ourselves? II Timothy 2:15 tells us, "Study to shew thyself approved unto God, a workman that needeth not to be ashamed, rightly dividing the word of truth." The Psalmist says, "Thy word have I hid in my heart, that I might not sin against thee." (Psalm 119:11)

We also need to keep in the Word to verify what we read and hear that comes from outside the Word. True, great wisdom comes from godly counsel. Preachers, teachers, evangelists, and the rest are all given to us by God for just that purpose, but they are just human and prone to making mistakes. There are also those out there with the intent to deceive. That's why we must verify. I John 4:1 states, "Beloved, believe not every spirit, but try the spirits whether they are of God: because many false prophets are gone out into the world."

Remember, sermons, devotionals, and commentaries are all well and good, but we should not neglect reading God's Word for ourselves.

KEEPING THE GOAL IN FOCUS

DO YOU EVER find yourself feeling overwhelmed by your circumstances? I know that I do. I certainly felt that way the last time I tried to clean up and rearrange my office. It seemed that every task I accomplished created three more. I felt as though I would never get done. Why was this? I was distracted by the multitude of tasks rather than remaining focused on the goal of a clean and better organized office and dealing only with the task immediately in front of me.

In our spiritual lives, we are to remain focused on Christ, as He is our ultimate goal. When we lose sight of that, becoming distracted by the cares and worries of our lives, we become overwhelmed. Just as I had to stop and refocus on the goal of a clean and organized office and concentrate on one task at a time rather than the multitude of tasks remaining, we should stop and refocus on Christ when we start to feel overwhelmed in our lives and work on the task that God has placed right before us rather than fretting about every detail that we can't possibly control.

Take therefore no thought for the morrow: for the morrow shall take thought for the things of itself. Sufficient unto the day is the evil thereof.

– MATTHEW 6:34

JESUS THE HERETIC

I WOULDN'T HAVE thought to call Jesus a heretic. In fact, the thought of doing so seems outright blasphemous. For all intents and purposes, though, a heretic is exactly what Jesus was. Don't get me wrong, I do believe there is such a thing as Biblical heresy, and that true Biblical heresy is indeed blasphemous against God and His Word. The term *heretic*, though, has a much broader application.

People have been labeled heretics for centuries because they merely went against established traditions, philosophies, and accepted religious practices of their day. A perfect example of this would be Galileo Galilei, who was branded a heretic because he opposed the accepted teachings of Aristotle in favor of the scientific truth he had discovered. In this regard, Jesus was no exception. He was almost always at odds with the standards and practices set forth by the religious authorities of His day. So, was Jesus a true heretic, preaching against the Word of God? Absolutely not, but He was considered heretical by His contemporaries because He challenged the accepted religious system in favor of God's truth.

PEARLS BEFORE SWINE

Give not that which is holy unto dogs, neither cast ye your pearls before swine, lest they trample them under their feet, and turn again and rend you.
— MATTHEW 7:6

THERE ARE A few blogs that I read on a regular basis that deal largely with apologetics. While it certainly can make for some interesting reading, and I see nothing wrong with being able to logically defend one's faith, I sometimes wonder if perhaps too much emphasis is put on arguing against atheism and evolution, or rather against atheists and evolutionists.

First, there is the evolution vs. creation debate. One thing that bothers me about this debate is the immediate assumption by most creationists who believe in the literal interpretation of Genesis 1 that anyone who believes anything else is an absolute atheist. This, in and of itself, isn't necessarily so. There are those who don't hold to a literal interpretation of Genesis but see it as a figurative interpretation that could be easily understood by the people of that time. They don't deny that God was in control of the whole process, but they don't accept it as literal for various reasons. Personally, I believe in the literal interpretation. The God I worship could have taken seven seconds to create the universe. The time frame is irrelevant. The important part is that God was the one who made it happen, and more importantly, that Jesus Christ was part of the process (Genesis 1 and John 1).

The second, and far more egregious, aspect of the evolution vs. creation debate is the fact that it frequently takes the focus off our primary purpose. We are not commissioned to spread the creation story. We are commissioned to go and spread the gospel of Jesus Christ. Jesus said that no man comes to the Father except by Him (John 14:6b), not that no man comes to the Father except that he acknowledges Genesis 1 to be literal truth.

Now about those atheists... Yes, they will die and go to hell if they don't change their minds and believe in God and the redemptive work of Jesus Christ on the Cross, just like everyone else. Also, just like everyone else, browbeating them with their flaws and spiritual shortcomings, which is typically what I see happen, isn't going to win them over. It seems to me that the tendency is to be a lawyer for Christ when it comes to dealing with atheists rather than a witness for Christ. A lawyer tries to defend or prove, whereas a witness just shares his own personal experience and lets those he shares with decide for themselves.

When Jesus sent His disciples out, He told them that if they were not received, they should shake the dust from their feet as they left town as a testimony against them (Luke 9:5). While we are to spread the gospel and truth to everyone, God is the one who opens the ears and heart of the individual. Many need to hear. How much time are we wasting spreading our pearls before swine when we could be reaching a new flock of sheep?

> *Go ye therefore, and teach all nations, baptizing them in the name of the Father, and of the Son, and of the Holy Ghost: teaching them to observe all things whatsoever I have commanded you: and, lo, I am with you always, even unto the end of the world. Amen.*
>
> – MATTHEW 28:19–20

GOT SPIRIT?

But the fruit of the Spirit is love, joy, peace, long-suffering, gentleness, goodness, faith, meekness, temperance: against such there is no law.
– GALATIANS 5:22-23

I N ONE OF my devotionals, there is an entry about the fruit of the Spirit that shed new light on the topic that I hadn't thought of before. It was something so simple, I'm almost ashamed I didn't realize it on my own. It also pointed out something that I have certainly been guilty of.

When we find ourselves lacking in an element of the fruit of the Spirit, we tend to pray for more of that element. I find I'm not very patient, so I pray for more patience. Joe finds he isn't very loving, so he prays for more love. Mary finds she doesn't have much joy, so she prays for more joy, and so on and so forth. The problem is that, as Christians, we are supposed to produce this fruit, not receive it.

Think of a farmer. The fruit he produces isn't given to him by someone else. Instead, he plants the seeds that yield the fruit he harvests. The fewer seeds the farmer plants, the smaller his harvest. The correlation here and in the devotional is that our short supply of spiritual fruit can often be linked to a short supply of the Spirit.

Please understand that there is no attempt to imply a lack of salvation, but we often become caught up in the routine of physical life and neglect our spiritual one. When this happens, we lose connection to the Holy Spirit. Just as farmers need seeds to grow successful crops, we need the Holy Spirit to produce spiritual fruit, and the only way to get more of the Holy Spirit is to spend time with God in prayer and studying His Word. Of course, it doesn't hurt to pray for more of His Spirit in our lives, either.

> *But seek ye first the kingdom of God, and his righteousness; and all these things shall be added unto you.*
>
> – MATTHEW 6:33

Being Thankful

It may seem trite, but the Thanksgiving holiday isn't just about food, family, football, and Friday sales at the mall. It's a time to reflect on all that God has done for us and express our gratitude. In other words, it's a time to count our blessings and do what the Bible says we should be doing all the time.

Thanksgiving should be more than just the fourth Thursday in November for us. It should be a way of life. Paul tells us in Ephesians that part of being filled with the Spirit is giving thanks to God for all things (Ephesians 5:15–21). The author of Hebrews indicates that our sacrifice of praise is to be our thanks to God (Hebrews 13:15).

With such importance placed on giving thanks to God, how is it that so many of us relegate it to only one day a year? The real question is: does that truly show gratitude? In the time between Thanksgivings, we should do our best to keep the spirit of Thanksgiving alive by giving thanks and expressing gratitude to God throughout the year.

Carry On?

OFTEN, WHEN WE set out to do something related to our Christian walk, we start off with fervor and enthusiasm, but as time marches on, we wear down and start to get discouraged and fed up with our apparent lack of progress, or in some cases, the drudgery of routine. Our nature is to back away and do something else, but is this what we should do? The answer may surprise you.

We must begin by examining why we started doing what we've been doing in the first place. Was it just something that we wanted to do, or were we genuinely called? If it was just something we wanted to do, then perhaps we need to go no further in looking for our answer. We should probably move on because we haven't been doing what we were called to do in the first place. I know from personal experience that nothing wears us out faster than doing what we want rather than listening to God and doing what He calls us to do.

Next, let's examine the reasons we are feeling tired and frustrated. If we are doing what God has called us to do, quite often, our frustration and lack of energy come from one of two sources, if not both: misdirected focus and a lack of personal replenishment. The first of these implies that we have shifted our focus from God and are merely going through the motions. The second often goes hand-in-hand with the first and is often the first to creep in without our even being fully aware of it. We get wrapped up in the task and forget to take time out for personal prayer and meditation. Quiet time is important, but when we get busy, even with God's work, we often get sidetracked and forget about it. If either of these conditions exist, simply pulling back to take a break and recharge is all that's needed to get back to work.

Another possibility for feeling rundown and frustrated is that we are holding on to a calling longer than God wants us to. This can happen either because we have grown comfortable with our current calling and are reluctant to change, or because we are so busy and distracted that we miss God calling us to something new. In either case, we must stop being disobedient and move on to the new thing that God has for us.

There is one last possibility. Perhaps we are doing exactly what God has called us to do, and he is still calling us to do it, and we are doing our best to stay focused on God and keep up with our quiet time, but other tasks and perceived obligations weigh us down. These other tasks need to be given the same scrutiny as our calling. Perhaps we are holding on to personal interests that don't align with the life God wants us to live, and though we have done our best to pay attention to God when it comes to our church work, we have held on too tightly to the reigns of our day-to-day existence. Only when we put our whole lives into God's hands and give up the things He tells us to leave behind can we truly give our all without getting weary.

> *But they that wait upon the LORD shall renew their strength; they shall mount up with wings as eagles; they shall run, and not be weary; and they shall walk, and not faint.*
>
> – ISAIAH 40:31

Debunking
Bumper Sticker Theology

I'M SURE MOST of us have seen spiritual bumper stickers. Some of them are accurate, but others are deceptive and propagate falsehoods. There are three that I specifically wish to address.

1. **If all else fails, read the instructions.**

   This saying is normally accompanied by a picture of a Bible. This one is the least problematic and could probably be considered bad advice rather than an outright falsehood; after all, where better to turn when you are having trouble making things work? The falsehood is the assumption that some part of "all else" might actually work. Some variations correct this by using *when* instead of *if*, but why go to the trouble of doing all the other stuff first? Perhaps a better correction for this bumper sticker would be, "*Since* all else fails, read the instructions."

   > *All scripture is given by inspiration of God, and is profitable for doctrine, for reproof, for*

correction, for instruction in righteousness: that the man of God may be perfect, thoroughly furnished unto all good works.

– II TIMOTHY 3:16–17

2. **God is my copilot.**

This is flawed, no matter how you look at it. On the simplest level, the copilot only takes over when the pilot can no longer fly the plane. This puts God second, which is a direct contradiction to the First Commandment. On a more practical level, the pilot and copilot merely fly the plane the way the navigator tells them to. In a very real sense, God doesn't pilot our lives; He's our navigator. We should base our actions on what God tells us. While we are free to choose whatever path we want, it just works out best when we follow His instruction.

And thine ears shall hear a word behind thee, saying, This is the way, walk ye in it, when ye turn to the right hand, and when ye turn to the left.

– ISAIAH: 30:21

3. **God doesn't believe in atheists, either.**

I've saved the worst for last. Last I checked, atheists are people, and therefore, part of the world—the lost world that we are to try and reach. Also, last I checked, John 3:16 starts off, "For God so loved the world..." not, "For God so loved everyone but atheists..." Based on this, God sent Jesus to die for the sins of atheists, too. If that's not acknowledgement, then I don't know what is. The fact that atheists choose not to believe in God is just that: their choice.

> *The Lord is not slack concerning his promise, as some men count slackness; but is longsuffering to us-ward, not willing that any should perish, but that all should come to repentance.*
> — II PETER 3:9

WHICH CAME FIRST?

JUST SO YOU can't say I didn't warn you, what you are about to read is an exercise in the absurd. I found it funny and thought that others might as well, and since it involves a discussion on... well, maybe just a slight mention of creationism, I decided to include it, even though it has little to do with any real measure of faith whatsoever. Of course, the rest of this tome is chock full of deep, serious contemplation of faith, so a bit of levity and silliness seems in order. (I'll let you decide how much of that previous statement is spot-on or tongue-in-cheek.)

There is a question that has plagued man as a paradox for quite some time: which came first, the chicken or the egg? Now, through nothing but the sheer power of reason, I am going to show you that this is not a paradox at all but instead has a relatively simple answer: both. Yes, I said both. Some of you are now looking at me as though I've lost my mind, and perhaps I have, but this is not proof of it. You will see that I am correct no matter what you believe, as I intend to argue my point from both secular and Biblical viewpoints.

Let's begin by defining the terms of the question. *First* is obvious in its meaning, as is *chicken*. Where we run into trouble is the term *egg*. Does this refer to eggs in general or specifically to a chicken egg? This is an extremely important question, as this is what determines which truly came first.

We'll start by defining *egg* to mean eggs in general. Many creatures lay eggs, not just chickens. From a Biblical view, it's quite possible, and more than likely, that the first animal to lay an egg was probably a fish or other bird rather than a chicken. From a secular viewpoint, several egg-laying animals came into being well before the chicken. As you can see, by just referring to eggs in general, the chicken was late to the party. The egg was undeniably first.

I have a decent idea of what you're thinking right about now. You probably want to say something like, "But anyone can plainly see that the word *egg* in the question refers specifically to chicken eggs, so what do you say about that? Besides, you said the answer was 'both' and that was clearly 'the egg'." Well, if the question refers specifically to chicken eggs, then the answer is that the chicken came first. Common sense tells us you must have a chicken to produce a chicken egg. An egg from another animal isn't a chicken egg. Again, from a Biblical viewpoint, God made the first chickens—at least a rooster and a hen—and then the hen laid the first chicken egg. From a secular point of view based on evolutionary theory, while the first "true" chickens may have hatched from eggs, those eggs came from something that wasn't a "true" chicken, so the first "true" chicken eggs were laid by those first "true" chickens, thus proving that the chicken came before the chicken egg.

Since I've now logically proven that eggs in general were around before the chicken and that chicken eggs weren't around until after the chicken was on the scene, and since just saying *egg* can be interpreted either way, the answer to the question is undeniably—at least in my mind—both.

An Abundance of Thanksgiving

THANKSGIVING HAS LONG been one of my favorite holidays, but one year in particular, the true realization of all I had to be thankful for came home in some rather pointed and unexpected ways: I was sick, my regular holiday travel plans were put on hold, and my car had issues. These may seem like odd things to be thankful for, but I guarantee these things definitely put the "giving thanks" back in Thanksgiving for me.

To begin, I'll address the horrible issue of the 24-hour stomach flu. I am not prone to getting sick in that manner easily. I may have a bit of an upset stomach from overeating on occasion, but seldom do I genuinely get outright ill. Aside from feeling like I wanted someone to just rip my gastro-intestinal tract out with a dull butter knife because it would have felt better, I had a 102° fever. So exactly where is there anything to be thankful for in all that? Well, there were two things: my wife didn't get whatever I had, and it only lasted the Wednesday before Thanksgiving.

Unfortunately, my illness meant we had to cancel our annual pilgrimage—every pun intended—to my wife's grandmother's abode. We did this to make sure that I was well before we went up and saw people, as we didn't want to share whatever it was that had affected me so adversely with anyone. Again, we were thankful that I was only sick on Wednesday, so we were able to reschedule for Friday. This delay made us even more aware of how thankful we are for the time we get to spend with our loved ones who are not near us physically. We were also very thankful that my wife was able to have the entire Thanksgiving weekend off, thus allowing us to be able to reschedule for Friday and Saturday instead of Thursday and Friday.

The trip up to see my wife's grandmother went well. We had no problems and found out that my "new" car could make the trip in less than a tank of gas, which is something our other car was just not quite up to, so we were thankful for that. On Saturday, however, things began to sour in the car department. The weather had grown a bit chilly, and she became temperamental to start. I simply wrote it off to the colder weather and higher elevation, but that was not the end of it.

We all went to breakfast and then stopped for gas. After stopping for gas, she wouldn't turn over at all. Fortunately, we had jumper cables. We found a kind soul willing to provide us with a jump, and we were off. I thought that this would surely be the end of it, but I was wrong yet again.

After going back to Grandma's house, we had plans to go over to see my wife's uncle, who lived in the same area. Before going there, however, Grandma wanted us to go to the cemetery, so we agreed. She drove her car, and we followed her out in ours. Once at the cemetery, my wife asked if she should leave the car running, and I said no. Sure enough, as we went to leave, the car wouldn't start. We tried to jump it using Grandma's car, but that didn't work.

I must admit that my immediate emotion was one of frustration and irritation, though it wasn't long before the thankfulness of having come in two separate vehicles was quite apparent. Grandma and I went to the nearest Walmart and bought a new battery and some tools while my wife stayed with our car so it wouldn't be towed. The next moment of thankfulness came when simply swapping the battery fixed the issue completely. I would love to say the story could end here, but there is one more detail to go.

The battery was slightly larger than the old one. I did make sure that I was buying the right type, but there were two styles listed, and this was the only one that Walmart had in stock. I'm guessing the other might have been smaller, but it didn't really matter. Due to the size difference, there was some difficulty getting the mounting bracket back in place, so we wedged it in as tightly as possible and went on about our day.

We had to leave town shortly after lunch and head back home. We decided not to tempt fate and kept the car running when we stopped since we knew we wouldn't have to stop for gas. After our third stop, I took over driving. Once back on the highway, I tried to set the cruise control. The dashboard went crazy, and the headlights started flickering on and off. About that time, I noticed sparks coming out from under the hood. My wife went out and investigated the problem instead of me because of the amount of traffic (her idea, not mine), and just as I had suspected, the mounting bracket had come loose and made contact with the positive terminal on the battery. We then pulled the car over as far as we could so that I could get out as well, and between the two of us, we managed to resecure the bracket firmly into place and had no further incidents. Our last bit of thanks came in knowing that we were able to quickly fix the problem that had developed and that no serious damage was done.

There was a time in both of our lives that a Thanksgiving weekend like this would have felt completely ruined, but because we were able to see God's blessings and were able to be truly thankful for them, even in the mist of difficult circumstances, we had one of the best Thanksgivings ever.

> *O give thanks unto the Lord, for he is good: for his mercy endureth for ever.*
>
> – PSALM 107:1

THE RATIONAL CHRISTIAN

WHY IS IT that rationality and skepticism are seemingly left to the realms of agnostics, atheists, and anti-theists? When did science and Christianity part ways? Why do we accept this model of one or the other, inevitably pitting intelligence and reason against faith and theology? The Bible tells us to think and reason and admonishes us to not take what others say as truth but compare it to Scripture to test its merit. If that isn't reasoning and being skeptical, I don't know what is.

There was a time when the greatest scientists of the day were all devout Christians. Johannes Kepler, Sir Isaac Newton, Galileo Galilee, et al. But now we are faced with most scientific minds, or at least those getting the most recognition, being those who not only don't accept Christianity, they deny the very existence of God as well. And for those who aren't scientists, both in the secular and Christian communities, there is a strong misconception that science is a belief system rather than a methodology for thinking, experimenting, and observing.

Admittedly, there is something about dealing with empirical data as closely as the scientific method requires that can lead to difficulty accepting anything that cannot be quantified or explained. At risk of sounding trite, however, that's why it's called faith. But having faith and believing in God don't preclude one's ability to reason. The difference is that instead of believing that everything came into being by happenstance, there is belief in a Creator that was in control of the process, and knowing the properties of light that allow water droplets and prisms to split it into the different colors of the visible spectrum does not diminish the miraculous nature of the rainbow.

As Christians, we still have brains and still need to use them. To do otherwise is wasting what God gave us and disobeying His Word. Don't just take my word for it, though. Look it up for yourself.

Get wisdom, get understanding: forget it not; neither decline from the words of my mouth. Forsake her not, and she shall preserve thee: love her, and she shall keep thee. Wisdom is the principal thing; therefore get wisdom: and with all thy getting get understanding. Exalt her, and she shall promote thee: she shall bring thee to honour, when thou dost embrace her. She shall give to thine head an ornament of grace: a crown of glory shall she deliver to thee.

– PROVERBS 4:5–9

Study to shew thyself approved unto God, a workman that needeth not to be ashamed, rightly dividing the word of truth.

– II TIMOTHY 2:15

All scripture is given by inspiration of God, and is profitable for doctrine, for reproof, for correction, for instruction in righteousness: that the man of God may be perfect, thoroughly furnished unto all good works.

– II TIMOTHY 3:16–17

DEBUNKING FACEBOOK THEOLOGY

ONE THING THAT constantly gets on my last nerve is the false theology that presents itself on Facebook. I don't know how much my ranting and railing about it is going to affect things, but if even one person takes heed to what I say, then perhaps I've done some good. In this spirit, I present to you the top four false doctrines that I see quite regularly on Facebook. This list is far from comprehensive, but most of what I see falls into one of these four categories.

1. **The "God is a genie, and this is how you rub the lamp to get your wish," post:**

   To quote a famous insurance ad, "That's not how it works! That's not how any of this works!" Prosperity gospel in all its forms is contrary to Scripture. No amount of typing "Amen" or sharing or liking will convince God to grant your every wish. God will answer earnest prayer, but prayer is not an incantation to make God do what we want.

2. **The "Push a button to show you're saved," post:**
    This is essentially what I discussed in "Christian Spam". In that post, I discussed how it presents a false gospel that something we can do can save us, and this is still true, but what I want to focus on now is another issue related to what Christ said about doing things in public vs. doing them in private. In the Sermon on the Mount, He discusses how the hypocrites do their alms in public so that everyone can see how awesomely religious they are. He also states that since they are seeking approval from men, they have their reward. He admonishes us as true believers to do such things in private so that God, who sees what we do when no one else is watching, may reward us openly (Matthew 6:1–6). At best, responding to these posts serves only the purpose of drawing attention to how supposedly spiritual and righteous we are, and at worst, as mentioned previously, it presents a false gospel that contradicts salvation by grace through faith.

3. **The "Believe in God because it's logical," post:**
    I'm certain that I'm personally guilty of saying something like the posts I'm referring to at some point in time, and I see nothing inherently wrong with being pragmatic about matters of faith, but the message that is typically thrown around is flawed and assumes that the only option besides Christianity is atheism. It goes something like this: "If I'm wrong about God, then I've wasted my life, but if you're wrong about God, then

you've wasted your eternity." To begin with, even if we as Christians are wrong, how is living a life where we die with a clear conscience and friends and loved ones who remember us fondly a wasted life? More importantly, the idea that if we as Christians are wrong, the worst that happens is that we die, and that's the end of it, is only true if the only other option is atheism. If we compare Christianity to other religions, then depending on the religion, the outcome of being wrong for either side is a wasted eternity. It takes more than flawed logic to support what you believe.

4. **The "Virtues of unanswered prayer," post:**
I've saved the worst offender for last. For Christians, there is no such thing as unanswered prayer. The Bible makes it clear that God hears the prayers of the faithful and answers them. The problem we have as people is that we, much like children, don't want to accept answers that aren't what we want to hear. "No," "Wait," and, "I have something else in mind," are all answers. Just because we don't get the answer we want or were expecting doesn't mean the prayer was unanswered.

STOP THE SHAME

A LL EMOTIONS ARE real, and sometimes the negative emotions are the ones that are overwhelming. If we keep them bottled up and suppressed and never deal with them, they can begin to eat away at us. While we shouldn't dwell in negativity, to deny the existence of negative emotions or pretend we don't feel them is equally wrong. There is nothing wrong with having negative emotions. Where we often run into trouble is in our responses to those negative emotions. The Bible says, "Be ye angry, and sin not..." (Ephesians 4:26a) Why would we be admonished against sinning while angry but told to be angry if anger—a negative emotion—was sinful all by itself? I believe it is possible to dwell too much on negative emotions, and obviously it is possible to act on negative emotions in a way that is inappropriate, but expressing and being honest about those emotions helps to work through them.

When we do express those negative emotions, there are plenty of people out there who want to come along and tell us that we should be focusing on the positive, looking for the good, remembering that others probably have it worse, and even more nonsense about not letting situations "steal our joy". While many of these individuals believe they are coming from earnest places of wanting to help, this kind of sanctimonious emotional piety seems to come from a self-righteous, holier-than-thou attitude and ultimately doesn't help to deal with the emotion at hand but rather shames the person going through the negative emotion into feeling guilty—yet another negative emotion—about having negative emotions. It seems a bit counterproductive, in my opinion.

If a person is acting on their negative emotions in a way that could harm themselves or others, then something should be done to intervene, but if all that is going on is someone expressing their feelings, let them work through it. Be there for that person, but leave the platitudes behind, and stop shaming negative emotions.

JESUS MAY NOT BE A REPUBLICAN, BUT HE'S NOT A DEMOCRAT, EITHER

I NORMALLY TRY to steer away from discussing politics, but I found a meme on Facebook that I couldn't let go unanswered. The meme had two pictures of Jesus, with WWJD above the picture on the left and WWRJD above the picture on the right. The left image was a typical icon-style depiction of Jesus, and the one on the right had been modified with a military-style rifle, a less-than-flattering GOP seal, an American flag bandana, and a stack of cash. Below the left image was a list of things that the creator of the meme suggested that Jesus would do: feed the hungry, care for the sick, shelter the homeless, and love everyone. It's hard to argue with that, since based on most of his teachings, this is, at least at face value, relatively accurate. But then we come to the image on the right and the list of things this "Republican Jesus" would do: cut food stamp benefits, gut affordable healthcare, demonize the homeless, and block equal rights. What the person who came up with this meme failed to realize is that just as this "Republican Jesus" apparently goes against everything that the real Jesus stands for, so does "Democrat Jesus". Jesus is neither Republican nor Democrat, so in the interest of balancing things out, here's a list of answers to the question, "What would Democrat Jesus do?"

- Demand the government come up with a program that takes money from hard-working citizens to feed the hungry while doing nothing to solve the problem himself.

- Demand the government require everyone to have "affordable healthcare", even though it ends up costing most people more money and results in those who can't afford it having to pay a fine for not having something they couldn't afford in the first place.

- Demand the government come up with a program that builds houses for those who don't work to be paid for by additional taxes on those who do, while sitting back and not helping non-profit organizations such as Habitat for Humanity that already do this.

- Require that the government undermine personal freedom and impose its own brand of preferential treatment because government-mandated discrimination is so much better than common, unregulated discrimination.

While Jesus may have fed the hungry, cared for the sick, and loved others, His message isn't about requiring the government to make people do these things. It's about Him being the way, the truth, and the life (John 14:6), and how we as His followers should be doing these things on a personal level, not a government-mandated level. The government can never legislate morality, and when it tries to do so, it undermines our liberties. The only way to truly do what Jesus would do is to personally strive to be like Him and "get our hands dirty" doing the work of the gospel. It isn't political; it's spiritual, and it's not the government's job; it's ours.

A Thought to Ponder

ERHAPS THE REASON many modern scientists deny the existence of God lies not in their inability to quantify, observe, or otherwise catalog and measure Him, but rather in their fear that acknowledging there is a God diminishes the significance of their work. Perhaps in their minds, admitting there is a God means having to dismiss all that is currently unexplainable as "That's the way God made it," thus removing the need to pursue the matter further.

II Timothy 2:15a states, "Study to show thyself approved unto God..." Acknowledging God in no way relieves us from our duties to learn as much as we can about the universe He created. Early scientists, such as Johannes Kepler and Galileo Galilei, understood this. Why has this changed? Science and faith are not, by nature, at odds with each other. The point of science is not to prove or disprove God's existence but rather to allow us to better understand how His creation works. Understanding creation does not diminish the importance of the Creator. The point of faith is not to undermine or bolster scientific discovery but rather to acknowledge God as being the one who established the truths we uncover through science.

VICARIOUS GENEROSITY

T HERE ARE AT least two companies—one sells socks, the other sells shoes—that use their corporate generosity as a marketing tool. Both companies talk about how, for every pair purchased from them, a pair will be donated to some needy individual or worthy organization. There is nothing wrong with this. I personally feel more businesses should be open about what charity they do and do more real charity that goes directly to the people in need; however, the fact they are using this as a marketing tool leaves room for something less admirable to happen: vicarious generosity.

Vicariousness is essentially experiencing something second-hand. Often, parents will try to relive fond memories of things they did as children by forcing their children to "enjoy" those same things. Sometimes it works; sometimes it doesn't go so well. Sports fans live out the excitement of the game by watching and following the careers of their favorite players rather than by participating in the sport. Not all vicarious activities are bad, but almost all fall short of first-hand participation, and generosity is no exception.

Before I continue further, let me state that there is nothing wrong with purchasing socks or shoes from these companies or products from any other company that openly states their charitable donations as part of their marketing. The problem is in thinking that purchasing from these companies alone is sufficient to be considered generous. Here's what I mean: Let's say I could buy a pair of socks for $5.00. That means I spend $5.00 plus tax and shipping, and the company sends me and some unknown needy individual a pair of socks. I feel "good" because I got the socks I needed and sent a pair of socks to someone in need; only I didn't send those socks. The company I bought the socks from did that. I haven't done anything generous. I was vicariously generous. I bought socks from someone I knew was going to be generous, so that I could feel as though I was generous without having to be generous.

Now let's look at another scenario. I still need socks. Instead of ordering these socks from the company that will give a pair of socks away for every pair purchased, I go to a local big-box retailer and buy a pack of five socks for $7.00. I put two pairs in my sock drawer and give three pairs to a local homeless shelter. It might have cost me more money, but I've gotten two pairs of socks out of the deal instead of just one, and I've performed an act of generosity first-hand that ultimately helps three individuals in need instead of just one.

Vicarious generosity requires no effort or sacrifice. You simply do something you were going to do anyway, and someone else does the work. True generosity is typically not convenient and often requires some kind of sacrifice, whether in time, effort, expense, or some combination thereof. In the example of the socks, the act of true generosity required that I take the time to deliver the socks to the homeless shelter and required that I give up something that was technically mine. By rights, all five pairs of socks were mine. In the first example, the company did all the legwork to make the donation happen, and I had to give up nothing. The socks sent to the individual in need never belonged to me in the first place. I only paid for the pair I received. It's the willingness to give freely from our personal resources that marks us as generous people, not our ability to buy something from a company that touts itself as being generous.

Again, I wish to reiterate that there is nothing inherently wrong with purchasing items from companies that are openly philanthropic, but hiding a lack of true personal generosity behind vicarious generosity is a grave mistake.

OF ENDS AND MEANS

L IKE IT OR not, we live in a results-driven world. At our schools, our jobs, and in many other aspects of our lives, we are judged not by the actions we take but by the results of those actions. Did we pass the test? Did we meet the goals set by our superiors? Did we manage to pay all the bills? Did we get our friends to come to church with us? And the list goes on. And while overly unscrupulous actions are frowned upon in most, if not all, of these arenas, a blind eye is often turned to ethically gray and ambiguous tactics, provided the desired outcome is achieved. But should this be?

Scripture tells us that "...all things work together for good..." (Romans 8:28b), but that doesn't necessarily mean that everything that happens is a good thing. It just means that God can use any circumstance to craft a good end to otherwise bad actions "...to them that love God, to them who are called according to his purpose." (Romans 8:28c) If the ends justify the means, then why does Jesus ask, "For what shall it profit a man, if he shall gain the whole world, and lose his own soul?" (Mark 8:36) The reality is that our actions matter. The same Scripture that gives us Romans 8:28 also gives us Proverbs 14:12, which states, "There is a way which seemeth right unto man, but the end thereof are the ways of death."

Our actions cannot save us, but our salvation should affect our actions. Even if the ends are not exactly what we were aiming for, it's better to act morally and ethically, maintaining a clear conscience, and come up a bit short than to sacrifice our integrity for the sake of the bottom line.

CONDEMNATION AND REDEMPTION

THE BOOK OF Obadiah is short. In fact, it's the shortest book in the Old Testament. It only has one chapter of twenty-one verses. Through the overarching vision against Edom, we are shown God's condemnation of the lost and the promise of salvation and blessing to those who believe in and worship Him. This contrast is summed up nicely in verses four and seventeen. The first shows judgment against Edom—the lost—and the second shows the promise of protection and restoration for the house of Jacob—the faithful.

> *Though thou exalt as the eagle, and though thou set thy nest among the stars, thence will I bring thee down, saith the Lord. ... But upon mount Zion shall be deliverance, and there shall be holiness; and the house of Jacob shall possess their possessions.*
>
> – OBADIAH 4 & 17

WHO'S IN CONTROL HERE?

I WAS ASKED, "To what degree have you been able to control the course that your life has taken, or is being in control of one's life just an illusion?" This is my best effort to answer that question.

When I look back over the course of my life so far, I can see where certain decisions I made had an impact on how my life turned out. I can also see where decisions I thought were big at the time ultimately made little if any noticeable difference. I also see a myriad of other incidents and changes in my life that seem to have no reason whatsoever, and I wonder if any of the seemingly insignificant decisions that I've made throughout my life led to those events. It's completely unclear which decisions really made the most difference, and that, in and of itself, is a rabbit hole for another day.

I do believe that we have free will and that we have control over our own decisions, words, and actions. That's about all we have control over, but I would say that we are definitely in control of those things; however,

91

I can see instances in my past where some things just seemed fated, such as my wife and I meeting in college.

Way back in the dark ages, when I was a young lad of 19 and heading off to college for the first time, I was considering a rather prestigious college, at least in my mind, which would have enabled me to live away from my parents for the first time. Things went well, but the cost of student housing on top of the higher tuition was too much of a burden, despite the scholarships I had qualified for. Ultimately, I made the decision to attend my second choice of schools, which was close enough that I could live at home.

During the same time, my wife-to-be was making plans to attend the same prestigious university that I was, and for similar reasons at nearly the same time, she ended up enrolling at the same school I had because she could commute from home.

Both of us made independent decisions that we were in control of, yet both of us seemed destined to be at the same school at the same time. So, are we in control? Again, I do believe that our choices are our own, but there seems to be some other force at work behind the scenes. This is the most obvious example that I have, but I've seen this kind of serendipity on multiple occasions in my life. Based on the idea that once is a fluke, twice is a coincidence, and three times is deliberate action, I can only assume that God is watching out for me. I don't know if this answers the question, but then I don't know that I can answer it.

THE POWER OF PURPOSE

WHEN MY FATHER-IN-LAW passed away, I inherited his stamp collection and a stack of floppy disks and thumb drives that contained portions of a book he had been working on. Stamp collecting was truly his passion, and this book was intended to be his masterpiece. I never expected him to finish it, but then I also expected that he would be working on it until he passed away rather than having health issues prevent him from working on it for the last few years of his life.

For better or worse, I decided that I needed to try and complete his book for him, or at least compile what he had written into something resembling a finished book. This, however, was not to be. Part of the issue was the condition of many of the disks. Several files were corrupted to the point that they could not be opened at all, and of those that could be opened, approximately 25% had corrupted portions that came across as gibberish. Of what remained, there were obviously missing segments and many restarts and duplicated files, but I still wanted to try and make something resembling a book from his work.

I tried multiple times to organize the fragments I had to work with into some logical order and then edit them into something that felt like a coherent and well-thought-out manuscript, but time and time again, I would stop and throw my vain attempt in the recycle bin. It took a full two years and more attempts than I can truly remember to come to the realization that there was a great flaw in my plan. My purpose was truly self-serving. I wanted to put together a finished work to show what a great son-in-law I was. It had nothing to do with honoring my father-in-law, though that was my claim.

Clarity of purpose came in two stages. The first was recognizing that the fragments were too incomplete and disjointed to be a truly polished and finished work. So, I shifted to simply putting the pieces in as logical an order as possible and correcting the grammar; however, I was still intent on taking out some of the more superfluous elements of my father-in-law's writing. It was after failing at even this process that I gained my second moment of clarity. Taking out what I considered superfluous elements effectively stripped my father-in-law out of his own work.

Finally, I decided to let his work stand, only cleaning up the more egregious grammatical errors but leaving all his unrelated ramblings and rabbit chasing in place, with no attempt to polish his work into something that it could never be. It was only at this point, with full acceptance of what my father-in-law created and no intent of my own beyond presenting what he had so lovingly crafted, that the task became something I felt I could accomplish. My true purpose was finally aligned with what I stated I was trying to do.

In much the same way, our spiritual life can stagnate when our purpose does not align with that of our Creator. We get bogged down in the worries and routine of everyday life, losing our focus on the higher calling we claim to be pursuing and imposing our own will on all we do rather than allowing God to shine through us. It is only when we realign our true purpose with what we claim our purpose to be, allowing God to work through us rather than hindering Him with our own selfish motives, that we begin to feel the weight of the cares of this world slough away and move forward on the path to which God has called us.

> *And thine ears shall hear a word behind thee, saying, This is the way, walk ye in it, when ye turn to the right hand, and when ye turn to the left.*
> – ISAIAH 30:21

THE END

OTHER WORKS BY
FRANK C. RAY, IV

Coffee & Philosophy: A Book of Poetry

More Coffee & Philosophy: Another Book of Poetry

www.ingramcontent.com/pod-product-compliance
Lightning Source LLC
LaVergne TN
LVHW011211080426
835508LV00007B/717